CIVILIZATIONS

OF AFRICA

THE
ZULU
OF SOUTH AFRICA

Christine Cornell

W
FRANKLIN WATTS
NEW YORK•LONDON•SYDNEY

This edition first published in the UK in 1997 by
Franklin Watts
96 Leonard Street
London
EC2A 4RH

© 1996 The Rosen Publishing Group, Inc., New York

Picture credits: Cover, p. 12 © E. A. Schneider; pp. 4, 11, 15, 16, 19, 20 by A. Elliot,
© McGregor Museum, Kimberley, South Africa; p. 7 © Jean Morris/McGregor Museum;
p. 8 © South Light/Gamma Liaison.

A CIP catalogue record for this book is available from the British Library.

ISBN 0 7496 2860 X

Printed in the United States of America

Contents

Who are the Zulu?

The **Zulu** people live in South Africa.
Most Zulu live in modern cities and towns.
Others live on small farms in the country.
Many still follow ancient Zulu **traditions**.

Many Zulu live in KwaZulu-Natal.
This is a province, or state, of South Africa.
It is very warm there.

◀ Many Zulu still follow the old traditions.
This woman is a potter. Her hat and
clothes show that she is married.

King Shaka

Nearly 200 years ago there was a Zulu king named Shaka. He was a brilliant military leader. Shaka and his army of 80,000 warriors conquered many other peoples. The Zulu empire was very large and powerful.

Until about 100 years ago, the Zulu fought against European **colonists** who wanted to take away their land. The Zulu fought hard, but in the end they were defeated.

Today, the Zulu king is Goodwill Zwelithini. ▶
Here he speaks to his people.

Apartheid

For most of this century South Africa was ruled by white South Africans.
Black people were not treated as equals.
They were kept apart from whites.
This was called **apartheid**.

Apartheid ended in 1994. Now South Africa is a democracy. The head of the country is President Nelson Mandela.

◀ Nelson Mandela (right) is the first black African to be President of South Africa.

Zulu leaders today

The Zulu king and his chiefs are still powerful. The Zulu believe that lions and leopards have special powers. To show how powerful they are, Zulu leaders wear leopard-skin cloaks and necklaces of lions' claws.

Today, many Zulu still follow their king. But they must also obey the laws of the government of South Africa. Obeying both chief and government is not easy.

At special events, Zulu chiefs wear ▶ leopard-skin cloaks and headdresses.

Work

In the past, the Zulu reared cattle. They had large herds. They loved their cattle and knew each one by name. The warm climate and rich soil of KwaZulu-Natal also made it good for farming.

But today there is not enough land for everyone to keep cattle or to farm. Many Zulu people now work in a city.

◀ Bigger cities mean less land for the Zulu to farm.
This woman works as a hairdresser.

13

Homes

Traditional Zulu homes were made of grass woven over a wooden frame. People had to bend to get through the low doorways.

The chief's house usually had big cattle horns above the doorway to show that it was an important house.

Today, the Zulu who live in **urban** areas usually have homes built of bricks or other materials.

In country areas a few Zulu still build grass houses, but most live in modern homes. ▶

Beadwork

Zulu women are famous for their beadwork. They make necklaces and anklets and decorate clothes with brilliantly coloured beads.

Each colour has a meaning. In some parts of KwaZulu-Natal white means love and purity. Black means loneliness and grief. Yellow means wealth. But in other areas the meanings may be different.

◀ By looking at the beadwork patterns, the Zulu know exactly where someone comes from.

Making music

The Zulu have many ways of making music. They use reeds or **quills** to make whistles. Reeds or animal bones are used for flutes. They make drums by stretching animal skins tightly across round, hollow pieces of wood.

Zulu singers, such as the group Ladysmith Black Mambazo, are known all over the world for their music.

Drums are played at important ceremonies. ▶
This man is a drum maker.

Ancestor worship

In the past, the Zulu worshipped their **ancestors**. They believed that when people died their spirit lived on. The spirits watched over their living relatives. The ancestors' spirits might come back to earth as snakes.

Many Zulu believe that their ancestors expect them to follow the Zulu traditions. If they don't, the ancestors may be angry and cause bad luck. Today many Zulu are also **Christians**.

◀ The king's sister on her way to her Christian wedding.

Diviners

A Zulu who thinks he or she has angered
an ancestor usually goes to a diviner for help.
Diviners have a special link to the ancestors.
They can tell what has upset them and
what should be done to please them.

Diviners also make medicines from plants
for anyone who is ill or worried.

Diviners wear strips of animal skin and
beads across their chests and brightly
coloured beads in their hair.

Glossary

ancestor Relative who lived before you.

apartheid System of government which keeps different peoples apart.

Christian Person who believes in the teachings of Jesus Christ.

colonists People who move to another country which is still ruled by the country from which they came.

quill The hollow stem of a bird's feather.

tradition Doing things in the same way as they have been done for many years.

urban Anything to do with a town or city.

Zulu A people who live in South Africa.

Index